Meet the
Group of Seven

David Wistow and Kelly McKinley / The Art Gallery of Ontario

Kids Can Press

To K.S. and J.S. — D.W. and K.McK.

Acknowledgements

Sincere thanks to Dennis Reid, chief curator at the Art Gallery of Ontario, and Lynda Jessup, professor in the Department of Art, Queen's University, for reviewing the manuscript for this book. We are also very grateful to Robert and Signe McMichael for so generously sharing their memories of the Group. Many thanks to all the galleries and their staff for their cooperation in providing images for this book. Special thanks to Kids Can Press, especially designer Karen Powers and editor Liz MacLeod who have made this book a work of art.

Text copyright © 1999 by David Wistow and Kelly McKinley
Edited by Elizabeth MacLeod
Designed by Karen Powers
Permission management by Lori Burwash

Kids Can Press acknowledges the support of the Ontario Arts Council, the Canada Council for the Arts and the Government of Canada, through the BPIDP, for our publishing activity. Canadä

Published in Canada by
Kids Can Press Ltd.
29 Birch Avenue
Toronto, ON M4V 1E2

Printed and bound in Hong Kong by Book Art Inc., Toronto

CDN 99 0 9 8 7 6 5 4 3 2 1

Cataloging in Publication Data

Wistow, David
   Meet the Group of Seven

ISBN 1-55074-494-1 (bound)

1. Group of Seven (Group of artists) - Juvenile literature. 2. Painting, Canadian - Juvenile literature. 3. Painting, Modern - 20th century - Canada - Juvenile literature. I. McKinley, Kelly. II. Title.

ND245.5.G7W57 1999   j759.11   C99-931789-X

Kids Can Press is a Nelvana company

Contents

Meet the Group

Franklin Carmichael

Lawren Harris

A. Y. Jackson

Frank Johnston

Arthur Lismer

J. E. H. MacDonald

Frederick H. Varley

Tom Thomson

Some people say that the Group of Seven formed in 1920. But you could say that the Group really began in 1911 when several talented artists began working for an art and design company in Toronto. They became friends because they were all painters who believed that the true spirit and character of Canada could be found in its northern lakes and trees. They also shared a love for travelling and exploring Canada's wilderness regions.

Soon these friends met other artists who felt the same way. All of them wanted to create paintings about their experiences of the Canadian landscape and to exhibit their work. Since their artwork was so different from the art other painters were creating, the seven artists decided to exhibit as a group. For their first exhibition in 1920 they called themselves the Group of Seven.

Some people who saw that first exhibition were excited by the way the Group used bright colours and rough brushstrokes. Others were shocked and horrified because they had never seen paintings like these before. It took years for many people to appreciate what these artists were doing.

Who were the seven artists in the Group? Franklin Carmichael, Lawren Harris, A.Y. Jackson, Frank Johnston, Arthur Lismer, J.E.H. MacDonald and Frederick H. Varley. They might have been the Group of Eight, but Tom Thomson, an artist they all admired, had died in 1917, three years before the Group was founded.

As members left the Group or died, new members joined, including A.J. Casson, L.L. FitzGerald and Edwin Holgate. From 1920 to 1931, the Group held eight exhibitions at the Art Gallery of Toronto, now known as the Art Gallery of Ontario.

Here's how Toronto looked when the Group first met in 1911.

Franklin Carmichael designed this symbol for the Group in 1920.

GROUP OF 7

The first Group of Seven exhibition was held at the Art Gallery of Toronto (now the Art Gallery of Ontario) in May 1920.

Here's the Group of Seven in about 1920. You can see (left to right) Varley, Jackson, Harris, non-member, Johnston, Lismer and MacDonald. (Carmichael is absent.)

What the Group Loved to Paint

The Group painted many different subjects — people, farms, towns and cities. But their favourite subject was landscapes of Canada, showing water, the seasons, skies and trees.

☜ Water

This painting, called *The Little Falls,* was created by MacDonald. Like others in the Group, he liked to paint the movement and colour of lakes, rivers and waterfalls.

☜ Seasons

Fall was the Group's favourite time to paint because the leaves on many trees are so brightly coloured then. In this work called *Credit Forks,* Casson emphasizes the brilliant colours by placing the warm yellow leaves against the cool blue sky.

Skies

The Group loved to paint sunsets and storms — times when the sky is the most dramatic. MacDonald's painting *October Shower Gleam* shows the heavy dark clouds of an approaching storm.

Trees

The Group liked to show the shapes and colours of different types of trees. In *Algoma Country,* Harris includes coniferous (evergreen) and deciduous trees (trees that lose their leaves in the fall).

Why Did the Group of Seven Paint Landscapes?

The artists in the Group of Seven believed that Canada's vast wilderness made it unique. Their passion for the rugged Canadian landscape took them to parts of Canada that most people had never seen. They painted pictures not only to show what these places looked like, but also to share what it felt like to be there and what was special about them. They felt that landscape paintings by other artists didn't accurately show the character of the Canadian land.

☞ This is a photo of what J.E.H. MacDonald saw in 1921 when he travelled to the Montreal River in northern Ontario.

☞ This is the painting he created, which he called *The Solemn Land*.

Why does the painting look so different from the photo? MacDonald is showing you what it was like for him to stand alone looking at this scene. He wants you not only to know what it was like to see the landscape, but also to feel the movement of the water and the clouds, to hear the sound of the wind and to smell the scent of the forest.

MacDonald also shows how you can see and feel nature constantly changing. He paints the water using small strokes of colour to show the wind rippling its surface. He paints big dark clouds that only allow a little sunlight to shine on the cliff. The sunlight on the ground moves as the wind blows the clouds. And as the clouds and light change, so do the colours.

The Solemn Land,
J.E.H. MacDonald

By putting the paint on thickly and roughly, MacDonald tells you about the textures of nature — the rugged rocks, the rippled water.

MacDonald also shows you the powerful forces of nature by emphasizing the patterns in nature. See how he simplifies the shapes of the hills and trees into circles and triangles? Then he uses dark colours to outline these shapes and make them look strong and bold.

Here is MacDonald's painting of the view that you see in the postcard below. He called it *Falls, Montreal River.*

This is a postcard of the falls on the Montreal River in Algoma (an area of northern Ontario) from about the time when the Group was painting there.

Life as an Artist

It isn't easy to become an artist. You have to study and practise for many years. Some members of the Group of Seven went to art school in England, France, Germany and Belgium. Others attended classes in Toronto and went sketching on weekends. Thomson never went to art school, but learned by watching his friends and experimenting on his own.

The Group of Seven didn't paint all the time. Most of them could only afford to paint on weekends and holidays. Because they didn't sell a lot of paintings, they had to work at other jobs to support themselves and their families.

When they were young men, five of the Group (Carmichael, Johnston, Lismer, MacDonald and Varley) worked at Grip Limited, a Toronto company that designed posters and advertisements. Several of them were also art teachers, and Thomson worked as a guide for people on camping and fishing trips. Harris was lucky — his family was rich so he didn't have to worry about money and could focus on painting.

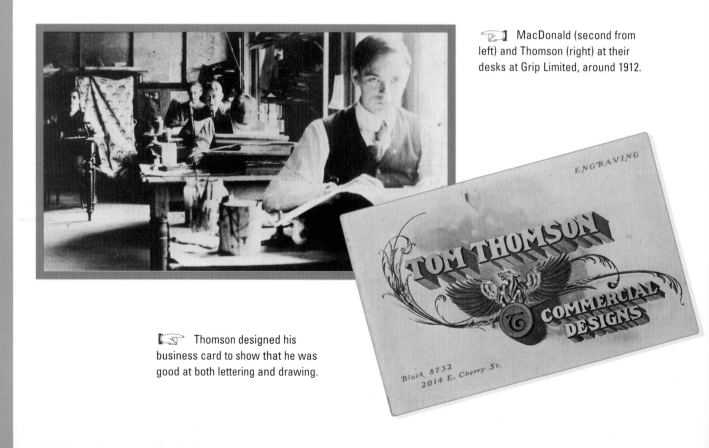

☞ MacDonald (second from left) and Thomson (right) at their desks at Grip Limited, around 1912.

☞ Thomson designed his business card to show that he was good at both lettering and drawing.

TOM THOMSON
COMMERCIAL DESIGNS
ENGRAVING
Black 8732
2014 E. Cherry St.

☞ Here are (clockwise from left front) Varley, Thomson, Jackson, Lismer and Lismer's wife Esther and daughter Marjorie on a painting trip to Algonquin Park in October 1914. The Group also especially liked painting around Georgian Bay and on the north shore of Lake Superior.

☞ Lismer was internationally famous for his ideas about teaching art to children. Here he is teaching a class outside the Art Gallery of Toronto in 1934.

☞ Freezing temperatures didn't stop Jackson from sketching outside on a trip to the Arctic in 1927.

☞ Lawren Harris is wearing a suit in this photo because he always wanted to look like a well-dressed gentleman, even when he was painting.

What Was So Different About Group of Seven Paintings?

Here are some paintings by the Group, together with works by artists who were painting before them. See for yourself how different they are.

Technique

☞ Allan Edson painted this way in the 1880s, and it was still popular in Canada in the 1920s. In *The Coming Storm, Lake Memphremagog* he used tiny strokes of paint to show every leaf and twig on the trees to create a painting as detailed as a photograph.

☞ Thomson, like all the members of the Group, was more interested in shape and movement than in detail. He used thick, swirling brushstrokes in *A Rapid* to show the movement of the water, and thick, long strokes to capture the shapes of the trees.

"Thomson's small oil sketches of the last years palpitate and throb. They are as direct in attack as a punch in the nose."

Harold Town, 1965

Subjects

☞ Landscape paintings of fields, animals and people, such as *Hay Making, the Last Load* by Homer Watson, were the type of pictures people were used to seeing at the time of the Group of Seven.

☜ The Group rarely included people or animals in their landscapes, as you can see in *North Shore, Lake Superior* by Carmichael.

☞ Detail from *Through the Rocky Mountains, a Pass on the Canadian Highway*

Ideas

Both Lucius O'Brien and Lawren Harris painted the Rocky Mountains. But each artist says something very different about them.

☞ In *Through the Rocky Mountains, a Pass on the Canadian Highway*, O'Brien has painted a steam engine crossing a gorge on a new railway bridge. The painting shows the pride and excitement people felt at discovering a way to travel across Canada quickly and easily, even through the highest mountains.

☞ Harris's *Isolation Peak* shows no traces of human beings. His painting is about the natural world and how it is more powerful and beautiful than anything people could make.

The Group from Coast to Coast

Most members of the Group of Seven called Toronto home, but they painted in all parts of Canada. They travelled great distances by train, boat, car and on foot.

☛ The Arctic

Harris's painting *Icebergs, Davis Strait* is based on a sketch he made during a two-month voyage to the Arctic with Jackson in 1930.

☛ Alberta

To find the best painting spot, Harris sometimes hiked 40 km (25 mi.) a day! *Maligne Lake, Jasper Park* is based on a sketch he made during a visit to the park with Jackson in 1924.

☞ Ontario

In 1920 Harris painted *Beaver Swamp, Algoma,* with its dead spruce trees drowned in a lake.

☞ Quebec

For 30 years Jackson returned each winter or early spring to Quebec to paint hills and old farm buildings, as you see in *Winter, Charlevoix County.*

☞ The Maritimes

Lismer's painting *Nova Scotia Fishing Village* captures his love for the sights and smells of Canada's east coast, where he went several times to sketch.

Painting in the North

Today you can go by car to a lake, mountain or provincial park. But 75 years ago, travel was much more difficult. There were no highways from Toronto to provincial parks — you had to take a train. And there were very few places to stay, so you had to camp.

Several times Lawren Harris arranged for the Group to borrow a boxcar (part of a freight train) that had been converted into a cabin with beds and a stove. The train company dropped off the boxcar and the members of the Group wherever they wanted to paint and then picked them up when they were finished.

 This paintbox was owned by Jackson. Since oil paint takes a long time to dry, the box was fitted with slots to keep sketches from touching each other and smudging. Paintboxes like this made it easy for members of the Group to carry their wet sketches on long canoe and hiking trips.

"In spite of the bad weather ... we have done a lot of work, got soaked pretty often too, but the boxcar is very cosy and one can soon get dried out ... The other chaps are all out sketching under umbrellas."

— Jackson, 1919

 Jackson, Johnston and Harris (left to right) on a boxcar trip through the Algoma region of Ontario in 1919. On one trip, Jackson couldn't paint with oils because mosquitoes kept getting mixed up in the paint.

Reasons to stay in Toronto and paint indoors:

- comfortable beds

- no worries about rain, snow or cold

- no need to carry heavy art supplies

- no bugs

Reasons to travel north and paint outdoors:

- exciting to be in nature

- see things, such as colours and shapes, as they really are

- no need to rely on memory or photographs (colour photos didn't exist then)

- no interruptions

Carmichael had to climb a hill to get the best view of Grace Lake.

When most members of the Group painted in Algonquin Park, they painted live, growing trees. But in this painting, *Northern River*, Thomson shows dead trees. He was attracted by the pattern of the black spruce branches against the sky.

In Lismer's cartoon *Beasts of Burden* you can see how heavy the Group's knapsacks were on their painting trips.

18 | How Did the Group Paint?

Many Group of Seven paintings are large — some as big as kitchen tabletops. It would be almost impossible to carry something this size through the woods or in a canoe. So the Group made small, quick paintings, called sketches, on thin wooden boards that fit into their paintboxes. (You saw Jackson's paintbox on page 16.)

Most artists sketch with pencils because they're easy to carry and use. However, the Group felt that colour was one of the most important features of the Canadian landscape and they knew it was impossible to show colour in a pencil sketch.

So the members of the Group used oil paint, which is thick and richly coloured, to express what they saw. Jackson and Harris often created both a pencil and an oil sketch of a scene. Since oil paint takes a long time to dry and smudges easily, they had to use special boxes to store and carry wet sketches so that they didn't get smeared on anything.

 Thomson painted this sketch in Algonquin Park in 1916.

The Jack Pine is the painting Thomson later completed in Toronto from the sketch. What changes did he make? Look at the colours and the brushstrokes.

Group members returned from their painting trips with many sketches, then enlarged the best ones into full-scale paintings. Lawren Harris had a special building built for the Group to paint in, called the Studio Building.

You can still see the Studio Building today beside the subway tracks near Yonge and Bloor Streets in downtown Toronto. Next to it was an old tool shed that Thomson converted into a studio and home for himself. It's now at the McMichael Canadian Art Collection in Kleinburg, Ontario.

Here's Jackson in 1965 on Baffin Island. In addition to his paints, brushes and boards to paint on, Jackson had to carry a folding stool so he wouldn't freeze sitting on the ground.

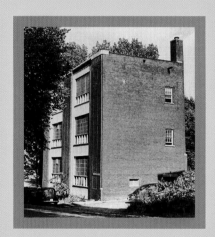

Artists need lots of light to paint well, so the windows in the Studio Building are large.

Not only did Jackson paint in the Studio Building, he also lived there.

The Mystery of Tom Thomson

Even though Tom Thomson was never a part of the Group, he was extremely important to it. He lived and worked in Algonquin Park for at least six months of every year, and he took his friends Jackson, Lismer and Varley on painting trips into the remote parts of the north that he knew so well. On these trips the artists developed the unique style that has made the Group so famous.

People still wonder whether Thomson's death was murder or an accident. Here are the facts:

- At approximately 12:50 P.M. on Sunday, July 8, 1917, Thomson went fishing on Canoe Lake.

- At 3:00 P.M. his overturned canoe was spotted floating upside down in the lake, not far from where he started. Friends began searching the nearby woods to find him.

- After ten days of searching, Thomson's body was found in the lake, about 115 m (375 ft.) offshore.

- When a doctor examined Thomson's body, he found a large bruise on the right side of his head, some bleeding from the right ear and copper fishing wire wrapped around one ankle. The doctor couldn't tell whether the injuries were the result of an accidental fall or an attack.

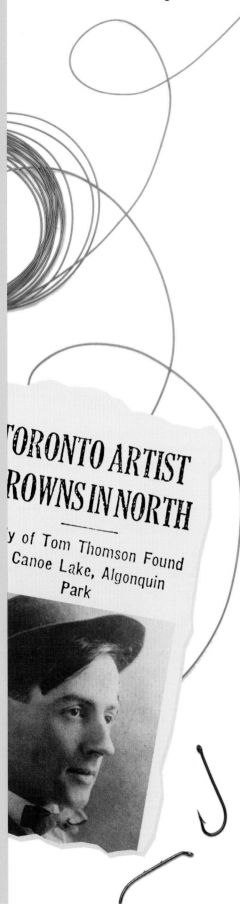

TORONTO ARTIST
ROWNS IN NORTH

y of Tom Thomson Found
Canoe Lake, Algonquin
Park

Thomson's *Autumn Foliage* can be seen as trees on a shore, but also as simply a pattern of colours and shapes.

Here are some theories about the mystery:

Murder?

Some people who knew Thomson were convinced he was murdered, because someone as skilled as he was in canoeing, fishing and navigating the lakes of northern Ontario would not have simply fallen overboard.

"Thomson could find his way over open water to a portage or a camp on a night as black as ink."

— Lismer, 1954

Other people thought that perhaps there was a fight and Thomson was pushed. He might have hit his head on a rock, which would have caused the bruise the doctor found. Others suggested he might have discovered some poachers (people who hunt illegally) and they killed him.

Accidental drowning?

Some people have said that Thomson might have stood up in the canoe and lost his balance. Perhaps he had had too much alcohol to drink and fell overboard. Or maybe a sudden wind or high wave tipped the canoe.

Suicide?

People wondered if Thomson killed himself, but there seems to have been no reason for him to have been that unhappy. To this day, no one knows for sure what happened.

What do you think?

 Thomson at Tea Lake Dam

 You can still see Thomson's monument at Canoe Lake, Algonquin Park. The inscription was written by MacDonald. Thomson's death deeply upset the members of the Group.

Painting a Portrait

The Group of Seven didn't only paint landscapes. Some of them liked to paint portraits (pictures of people). Just as Group members tell you stories about nature through their landscape paintings, they also tell stories about people and their lives by painting portraits, including portraits of themselves. As well, sometimes people would pay to have their portraits painted, which was a good way for Group members to make some extra money.

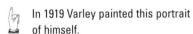 In 1919 Varley painted this portrait of himself.

"As you look at the sitter you see the truth emerging in the face. All people are beautiful in one way or another."

—Varley, 1959

Vera Wetherbie was a student of Varley. Some people think he was in love with her. In this painting *Vera*, Varley expresses his close relationship with her by focusing on her face, especially her beautiful eyes and lips.

 In this self portrait, Lismer has purposely included many details of his studio to show you how important making art was in his life.

Varley hardly knew Vincent Massey. In *Portrait of Vincent Massey*, Varley does not focus on the face as he did in the portrait of Vera Wetherbie. Varley paints Massey from further away, seated sideways, looking away. It's as if Massey isn't aware of either the artist or you and is preoccupied with more important business. Massey came from a very wealthy and important Toronto family. He was a businessman, a politician and the first Canadian-born governor general of Canada. Varley uses details such as Massey's serious expression and stiff posture to emphasize his important status.

This lumberjack was the best axe-handler in the Laurentian Hills, an area north of Montreal. In *The Lumberjack*, Holgate painted him with a serious expression to tell you how dangerous a lumberjack's job is.

Other Group of Seven Projects

The Group used their talents in many different art projects.

Advertising

☞ Carmichael designed this magazine advertisement for cars in 1926.

☞ This war poster was created by MacDonald in 1914.

Books

☞ In 1912 Jackson drew this cover for a book of children's songs. MacDonald also created illustrations for books.

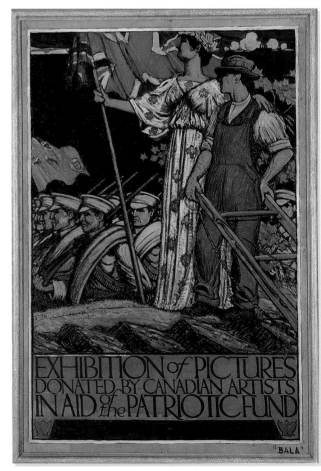

Cottage walls

☞ Jackson, Lismer, MacDonald and Thomson painted murals to decorate the walls of a friend's cottage on Georgian Bay. You can now see them at the National Gallery of Canada in Ottawa.

Train interiors

☞ This mural for the interior of a Canadian Pacific Railway passenger car was painted by Jackson in 1955.

Church ceilings

☞ St. Anne's Church in Toronto hired Carmichael, MacDonald and Varley to paint ceiling decorations in the church in 1923. These paintings are some of the largest the artists ever created. They painted them in their studios, then glued them to the church ceiling.

Did You Know ... ?

Thomson sold *A Northern Lake* to the Ontario government for $250. It was his first large painting and he asked for the payment in one-dollar bills so he could see just how much money it really was.

 MacDonald designed a special stamp to mark every sketch left in Thomson's studio after he drowned. This helps art experts today figure out which Thomson sketches are real and which are fakes.

 This is a forgery (a fake) of a Thomson sketch.

... Jackson started to work full-time at age 12 as an office boy in a printing company?

... Group of Seven members rented out their paintings to make money?

... Thomson's painting career lasted only five years? Despite that, he has become one of Canada's best-known artists.

... in 1920 a family could survive on $16 a week? One of the Group's paintings sold for $300 that same year. Today it might sell for as much as a thousand times that.

... Thomson was so poor that he used the wood from old orange crates to paint on? Sometimes he painted on both sides.

Jackson enlisted in the Canadian army in 1915. He fought in World War I and was wounded in the hip and shoulder.

☞ Varley used his thumbprint together with his signature to identify his paintings. Can you see his thumbprint signature in the bottom right corner on this portrait, *Head of a Girl*?

… MacDonald travelled long distances on his painting trips? Between 1920 and 1932 he probably journeyed over 58 000 km (36 000 mi.).

… Harris was the only member of the Group to attend university?

… Casson, Harris, Jackson, Johnston, Lismer and Varley are all buried at the McMichael Canadian Art Collection in Kleinburg, north of Toronto?

☞ FitzGerald painted *Doc Snyder's House* in Winnipeg during the winter of 1931. The winters are so cold there that he had to paint in a small shack that had a wood stove inside. The shack was on runners so FitzGerald could move it around.

Differing Opinions About the Group

When the Group of Seven first exhibited their art, people either loved it or hated it. It took several decades before the Group of Seven became Canada's best-loved artists. Here's what some people said about them when they first began exhibiting.

 The public would have found Harris's *Lake Superior* shocking because of its unnaturally smooth and simple shapes.

"Are These New Canadian Painters Crazy?"
— Canadian Courier, 1920

"The work of these young artists deserves enthusiastic recognition and support ... In their work the spirit of young Canada has found itself."

— Toronto Mail, 1919

"CRUELTY TO LANDSCAPE"
— Toronto Star Weekly, 1926

"The HOT MUSH School ...
the net result being more like a gargle or a gob of porridge than a work of art." — Toronto Daily Star, 1913

 The rough paint and strong colours of Jackson's *Terre Sauvage* appeared ugly and unnatural to many people when the painting was first exhibited.

"Young men seek to interpret Canada in original manner." — Mail and Empire, 1920

☞ When the art critic Hector Charlesworth saw MacDonald's painting *The Tangled Garden,* he wrote, "J.E.H. MacDonald certainly does throw his paint pots in the face of the public but it is a masterpiece compared with *The Elements* which might just as well be called Drunkard's Stomach or Hungarian Goulash."

☞ *The Tangled Garden,* J.E.H. MacDonald

☞ *The Elements,* J.E.H. MacDonald

☞ Here's Lismer's cartoon of Hector Charlesworth.

"... there were two dozen lakes, many of them not on the map. For identification purposes we gave them names. The bright sparkling lakes we named after people we admired like Thomson ... to the swampy ones, all messed up with moose tracks, we gave the names of the critics."

— Jackson, 1919

"Seven Painters Show Some Excellent Work."

— Toronto Star, 1920

"If we are to encourage immigration to this country, our federal government would be well advised to prevent some of the hideous paintings that are supposed to represent Canadian scenes from being shown abroad."

— Toronto Daily Star, 1930

What Do People See in Works by the Group of Seven?

 J.E.H. MacDonald

 Tom Thomson (right) with Arthur Lismer in Algonquin Park, 1914.

Everyone finds different meanings in works of art. There is no single correct meaning or interpretation. The artist may have one message, but everyone who sees a work discovers something different in it. Even curators, experts who study and care for works of art in art galleries, often disagree on what a painting means.

Take for example MacDonald's *The Beaver Dam*. Dennis Reid, chief curator at the Art Gallery of Ontario, believes the painting has two important messages. The canoe is a symbol of Tom Thomson, who drowned in 1917 while out canoeing. The beaver dam is a symbol of how fragile the natural environment is. For example, the dam is made of just tree branches and twigs, but it stops the river. However, the dam could break at any moment and the scene would change completely.

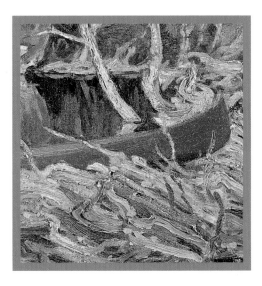

 Detail of *The Beaver Dam*, J.E.H. MacDonald

Lynda Jessup, a professor in the Department of Art at Queen's University in Kingston, Ontario, interprets the painting differently. According to her, the canoe gently reminds us of the presence of humans in the landscape. Delicately balanced on the beaver dam and surrounded by the quiet forest, it suggests that humans and nature can exist together in harmony, neither one controlling the other.

Here's how the painting makes other people feel:

"It reminds me of my childhood, playing with my brothers at the beaver dam. I can smell the stagnant water from the mud, leaves and branches."

"This painting makes me uncomfortable and uneasy. I feel as if I am an intruder on the peacefulness of the dam."

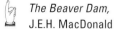
The Beaver Dam,
J.E.H. MacDonald

"This picture makes me feel warm and cosy. This painting brings back memories of camping trips."

What does the painting mean to you?

Other Artists of the Time

Here are Emily Carr and her pets in about 1931.

Many Canadian artists who painted at the same time as the Group were friends of theirs and even exhibited with them.

Emily Carr (1871–1945) was a close friend of Lawren Harris. She dedicated her entire life to painting landscapes such as *Scorned as Timber, Beloved of the Sky.* The rainforests and aboriginal villages of British Columbia were her favourite things to paint, and her images are as powerful and beautiful as the paintings of the Group.

It wasn't easy to be a woman artist at that time. A woman was expected to marry and look after her husband and children, but Carr chose to live alone and paint. As a result, people thought she was strange — they didn't understand her or her paintings.

Like the artists in the Group of Seven, **David Milne** (1882–1953) loved to paint outdoors. In *Painting Place, No. 3* you can see that he used less colour and more black and white than members of the Group did.

Scorned as Timber, Beloved of the Sky, Emily Carr

Painting people was what most interested **Paraskeva Clark** (1898–1986). She sometimes used her paintings to talk about the politics of the day. In *Petroushka* she shows workers watching a puppet show in which a rich man and a policeman are beating a poor man. When she created this painting, many people were fighting for the rights of the poor.

Bertram Brooker (1888–1955) was interested in painting abstract works, such as *Sounds Assembling*. His pictures are about shapes, space and colour rather than people and landscapes.

Frances Loring (1887–1968) liked to sculpt people in plaster, wood and stone. *Goal Keeper* is larger than life-size and is made of painted plaster.

Learn About Nature with the Group of Seven

 Stormy Weather, Georgian Bay, Frederick Varley

 Tamaracks, Tom Thomson

Artists have to take a lot of time to study and understand their subject if they want to paint it well. When the members of the Group of Seven painted images of Canada, they carefully studied nature and the environment — the weather, seasons, sky and trees. The Group believed that a landscape included sky, wind and weather, as well as the land itself.

You can learn a lot about nature and geography by looking at works by the Group of Seven.

Trees

You can identify many kinds of Canadian trees in the paintings of the Group of Seven.

Jack pines can survive without much soil and so are often found in bare, rocky landscapes, as you can see in *Stormy Weather, Georgian Bay* by Varley. You can usually recognize jack pines by their twisted and lopsided shapes caused by Canada's strong west winds.

Tamaracks are the only conifer that change colour and lose all their needle-like leaves in autumn. You can see how strongly coloured they can become in *Tamaracks* by Thomson. The trunks of tamaracks grow straight and tall and so are often used as telephone poles.

Sky

The Group of Seven paid a lot of attention to skies and weather. Often their landscape paintings focus on the sky rather than on the land. You can identify many different cloud formations and special light effects in their paintings.

The heavy and dense clouds in Thomson's *Grey Sky* are called cumulonimbus. They float low in the sky and cause thunderstorms.

Altocumulus clouds are the puffy, white clusters of clouds layered into lines in Johnston's *The Fire Ranger*.

Thomson's *Northern Lights* shows the aurora borealis (northern lights), the white, green, red and purple lights that move in patterns across the sky over northern countries.

Wind

The prevailing, or strongest, winds in Canada blow from west to east. Many artists provide clues in their paintings as to which direction the wind is blowing — the hints are in the ripples in the water, or the bends in the trees.

 Grey Sky, Tom Thomson

 The Fire Ranger, Frank Johnston

 Northern Lights, Tom Thomson

If the wind is blowing from west to east in this painting, *The West Wind,* can you figure out what direction Thomson was facing when he painted it?

(He was facing south.)

Landscape Art Since the Group

The Group of Seven split up in 1933 but many artists continued to be inspired by the Canadian landscape. Just like the Group, they looked for new ways to express their experiences and ideas about Canada.

☞ **Jack Chambers** (1931–78) grew up in London, Ontario. In *Lombardo Avenue,* he shows us how much he likes his city and how well he knows it by carefully recording every detail of the world around him. His painting almost looks like a photograph.

☞ Views of New Brunswick are what **Alex Colville** (born in 1920) loves to create. But he's most interested in showing the quiet, everyday lives of people and their pets, as in *Woman, Dog and Canoe.*

copyright 1973 Paterson Ewen

☛ **Paterson Ewen** (born in 1925) sees Canadian land as more than just trees, rocks and water. In *Northern Lights,* he portrays Canada as part of a larger and more complicated landscape — the universe.

☛ Many of **Gershon Iskowitz's** (1921–88) pictures, such as *Little Orange Painting II*, were inspired by the patterns and shapes he saw while flying over parts of Manitoba in a helicopter.

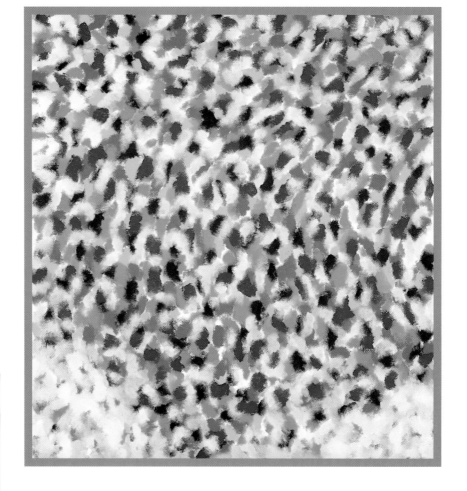

☛ **Iain Baxter** (born in 1936) was part of a group of artists who called themselves N.E.Thing Co. They felt that art could be made out of anything. Baxter's work *Bagged Landscape with Water* is made out of plastic filled with air and coloured water.

Remembering the Group

In the Caledon Hills, just northwest of Toronto, live Robert and Signe McMichael, the best-known collectors of paintings by the Group of Seven. The couple knew all the members of the Group except MacDonald (and Thomson), and they have lots of stories to tell about them.

"It was after we bought our first painting by the Group of Seven in 1953, Lawren Harris's *Montreal River,* that we became hooked on the Group of Seven," remembers Robert McMichael. "We didn't know any of the artists at that point. So I just began phoning them or writing them letters, saying that I loved their work and would really like to meet them.

 Robert and Signe McMichael

 Montreal River, Lawren Harris

"I think it was Lismer whom I met first. I dropped in on him in Montreal when I was there on business. But it was Jackson who we knew best. He lived with us for seven years before he died.

"Johnston was really the only member of the Group who was able to support himself by selling his pictures. Jackson was jealous of artists like him who were able to sell lots of paintings. So Jackson decided to paint pictures that didn't look like they were by the Group of Seven.

"As a joke, Jackson signed the pictures 'Zuppa,' which is Italian for soup. He took them to Eaton's in downtown Toronto and they sold instantly, no question about it. Probably under the name Jackson, no one would have been interested in them."

Often Lismer had to canoe to the remote sites he wanted to paint.

The McMichaels bought this painting, *Pine Wrack* by Lismer, in the 1950s. Wrack means something that has been twisted and destroyed by the weather.

"Lismer was so modest when I asked him how much his pictures cost. He'd make me play a little game because he was too shy to say the price out loud. Lismer would write a price on the back of each picture. I would then choose the pictures I liked best.

"Then Lismer would look on the back of these pictures and I would pay him half of what he had written there. I think I bought about a dozen."

— McMichael, 1998

So You Want to Own a Group of Seven Painting

The best way to buy a painting by the Group is to go to an art auction, a kind of sale where the person who is willing to pay the most for a painting gets it. The price depends on what kinds of paintings are popular at the time.

The highest price ever paid at an auction for a Group of Seven painting is $1,056,000 for *Lake Superior III* by Harris. That's a bargain compared to the highest price ever paid for any painting, which is $102 million for one by Vincent van Gogh.

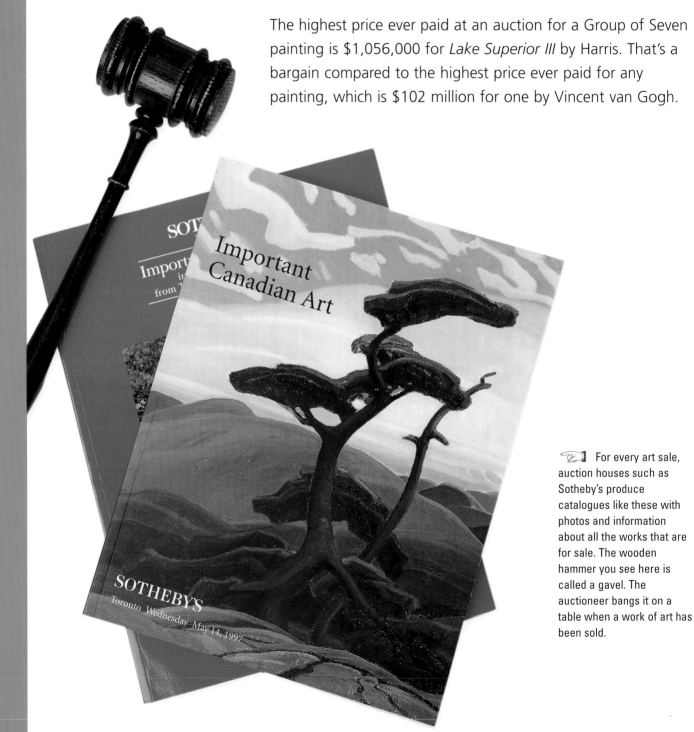

For every art sale, auction houses such as Sotheby's produce catalogues like these with photos and information about all the works that are for sale. The wooden hammer you see here is called a gavel. The auctioneer bangs it on a table when a work of art has been sold.

Once you've bought your painting, you have to look after it carefully. As paintings get older, they get dirty from dust, fingerprints and air pollution. Since the dirt builds up very slowly over many years, you may not notice just how dirty the paintings are.

For instance, when staff at the Art Gallery of Ontario looked at Harris's painting *The Corner Store* under a microscope, they discovered it was covered with coal dust and nicotine, which made the colours look dark and dull.

Like all paintings, this one had to be cleaned very slowly and carefully so as not to damage the old paint. An expert known as a conservator used cotton swabs with many different cleaning liquids to remove the dirt, as well as a layer of varnish that had gotten darker. Working in sections about the size of a Loonie, she took an entire week to clean this painting.

If you own a painting, you have to be careful not to touch it. No matter how clean your fingers seem, they're covered in dirt and natural oils that can soil a painting. You should also be careful not to leave the painting in bright light. Light and heat will damage the paint and canvas over time. Remember that paintings are original, one-of-a-kind works of art that can never be replaced.

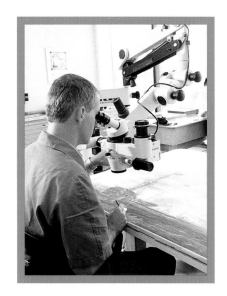

 The Art Gallery of Ontario employs a team of conservators who are responsible for preserving and cleaning the gallery's collection of artwork. They are specially trained in art and chemistry.

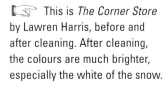 This is *The Corner Store* by Lawren Harris, before and after cleaning. After cleaning, the colours are much brighter, especially the white of the snow.

Before cleaning

After cleaning

The Artists

Franklin Carmichael
(1890–1945)

Born in Orillia, Ontario, Carmichael trained as a commercial artist at Grip Limited, the Toronto design company where Johnston, Lismer, MacDonald, Thomson and Varley worked. Carmichael mostly painted on weekends and on vacations. Two of his favourite subjects were Ontario villages and the La Cloche Hills along the north shore of Georgian Bay. Unlike most other Group members, Carmichael often painted in watercolours.

Alfred Joseph Casson
(1898–1992)

In 1926 Carmichael invited Casson to join the Group of Seven as a replacement for Johnston, who had left. Carmichael played an important role in Casson's life, training him as a commercial artist and encouraging him to paint in his spare time. Casson never painted outside Ontario. He's best known for his watercolour paintings of the province's small towns.

Lionel LeMoine FitzGerald
(1890–1956)

FitzGerald was the last member to join the Group of Seven. Like other members of the Group, he couldn't afford to paint full-time so he worked as a commercial artist, a teacher and an interior decorator. FitzGerald spent his whole life in Winnipeg, Manitoba, and liked painting images of things that were familiar to him — his backyard, his neighbourhood and objects in his home.

Lawren Stewart Harris
(1885–1970)

Harris is thought of as the leader of the Group of Seven. He came from a wealthy Ontario family so he was able to devote his whole life to painting and encouraging other Canadian artists. He built art studios for the Group and paid for some of their trips to the north. Harris's paintings are the most varied in subject. He painted not only wilderness landscapes but also views of Toronto, portraits and abstract designs.

Edwin Holgate
(1892–1977)

Holgate joined the Group of Seven in 1931. He had trained in Paris but lived and worked in Montreal. Although Holgate went on landscape sketching trips with Jackson in British Columbia and Quebec, he is known primarily for his paintings of people. Holgate had many different art-related jobs in his life, including war artist, teacher and mural painter.

Alexander Young Jackson
(1882–1974)

Born in Montreal, Jackson trained as a painter in Chicago and Paris. In 1913 he moved to Toronto where he met Thomson, who encouraged him to paint in Algonquin Park. Jackson joined the army in 1915 and painted scenes of World War I in Europe. He was Canada's most travelled artist and painted in the Arctic, British Columbia, Alberta, Ontario and the Maritimes. Jackson's favourite subjects were the farms and villages of Quebec.

Frank Johnston
(1888–1949)

Toronto-born Johnston worked as a designer and studied art at night. In 1918 he joined Harris and MacDonald on the first boxcar trip to Algoma, the area of Ontario he liked best. Shortly after, he became the principal of the Winnipeg School of Art. Johnston exhibited with the Group of Seven only once, at their first exhibition in 1920, then left the Group in 1924. But he continued to paint and, unlike the work of other members of the Group, his paintings sold well.

Arthur Lismer
(1885–1969)

Lismer was born in Sheffield, England, and studied art in England and Belgium. When he came to Canada, he got a job at Grip Limited in Toronto. As well as being a painter, Lismer was a world-renowned children's art teacher, and in 1933 he started the Children's Art Centre in Toronto. Lismer liked to paint around Georgian Bay and Algonquin Park. He especially enjoyed painting subjects such as fishing villages and plants in the forest.

James Edward Hervey MacDonald
(1873–1932)

At age 14 MacDonald immigrated to Hamilton, Ontario, from England. Thanks to his art training, MacDonald worked as a book illustrator, art teacher and painter. He also decorated a church, an office building and an apartment building lobby. MacDonald spoke and wrote well and often defended the Group's work and aims. He is best known for his paintings of Algoma, an area west of Sault Ste Marie, Ontario.

Tom Thomson
(1877–1917)

Tom Thomson grew up on a farm near Owen Sound, Ontario, and worked in Toronto designing advertisements. In 1914 he quit to do what he loved best — paint the Canadian wilderness. From early spring to late fall Thomson camped, fished, canoed and painted across Algonquin Park and Georgian Bay, often joined by the artists who would become the Group of Seven. Thomson drowned in Canoe Lake, Algonquin Park, in 1917, three years before the Group was formed.

Frederick Horsman Varley
(1881–1969)

Varley was born in England and, following the suggestion of Arthur Lismer, moved to Toronto at the age of 31. After studying art in England and Belgium, he worked as a commercial artist and art teacher. Varley was also an official war artist. He never made a lot of money and had a difficult time supporting his family. As a landscape painter, Varley loved the mountains around Vancouver most, but he's best known for his portraits.

Group of Seven Time Line

1920	The Group forms.
1924	Johnston leaves the Group.
1926	Carmichael invites Casson to join the Group.

1931	Holgate joins the Group.
1932	FitzGerald joins the Group.
1933	The Group breaks up and a new association, called the Canadian Group of Painters, is formed.

Credits

Meet the Group (pages 4/5)

For credits for portraits on page 4, please see credits for pages 42/43 and 44/45

Toronto in 1911
City of Toronto Archives; SC 244-491

Catalogue cover for the first Group of Seven exhibition (May 7–27, 1920) (detail)
McMichael Canadian Art Collection Archives

First Group of Seven exhibition at the Art Museum of Toronto (May 7–27, 1920)
McMichael Canadian Art Collection Archives

Group of Seven: Luncheon, Arts and Letters Club, Old Court Lane Premises
National Gallery of Canada, Ottawa

What the Group Loved to Paint (pages 6/7)

Maple leaves
David Wistow

MacDonald, J.E.H. Canadian 1873–1932
The Little Falls, 1918
oil on board; 21.6 x 26.7 cm
Art Gallery of Ontario, Toronto
Purchase, 1933; 2106

Casson, A.J. Canadian 1898–1992
Credit Forks, c. 1930
graphite and watercolour on wove paper; 46.6 x 56.8 cm
Art Gallery of Ontario, Toronto
Gift from Friends of Canadian Art Fund, 1930; 1327

MacDonald, J.E.H. Canadian 1873–1932
October Shower Gleam, 1922
oil on canvas; 122.5 x 137 cm
Hart House Permanent Collection, University of Toronto

Harris, Lawren S. Canadian 1885–1970
Algoma Country, 1920–1921
oil on canvas; 102.9 x 127.5 cm
Art Gallery of Ontario, Toronto
Gift from the Fund of the T. Eaton Co. Ltd. for Canadian Works of Art, 1948; 48/9

Why Did the Group of Seven Paint Landscapes? (pages 8/9)

Pine bough
David Wistow

Detail from Algoma
Photo: Thoreau MacDonald (?)
McMichael Canadian Art Collection Archives

MacDonald, J.E.H. Canadian 1873–1932
The Solemn Land, 1921
oil on canvas; 122.5 x 153.5 cm
National Gallery of Canada, Ottawa
Purchased, 1921; 1785

Montreal River near Sault Ste. Marie, Ont.
postcard
David Wistow Collection

MacDonald, J.E.H. Canadian 1873–1932
Falls, Montreal River, 1920
oil on canvas; 121.9 x 153 cm
Art Gallery of Ontario, Toronto
Purchase, 1933; 2109

Life as an Artist (pages 10/11)

Tools used by graphic artists
Photo credit: Sean Weaver, Art Gallery of Ontario

J.E.H. MacDonald, Tom Thomson and Harold James at Grip Ltd., c. 1912
Archives of Ontario; F 1140 s.2791

Tom Thomson
Business card, Seattle, c. 1903
Location unknown
Photograph courtesy of Joan Murray
Tom Thomson Papers

Algonquin Park, October 1914
National Gallery of Canada, Ottawa; 15-4-80

Arthur Lismer with spring sketching group in Grange Park, 1934
Photo Credit: City of Toronto Archives
Courtesy Art Gallery of Ontario

A.Y. Jackson sketching in the Arctic, 1927
McMichael Canadian Art Collection Archives
Reproduced courtesy of Dr. Naomi Jackson Groves

Lawren Harris painting in a suit
National Gallery of Canada, Ottawa

What Was So Different About Group of Seven Paintings? (pages 12/13)

Allan Edson Canadian 1846–1888
The Coming Storm, Lake Memphremagog, 1880
oil on canvas; 60.6 x 106.8 cm
Collection Musée du Québec (59.577)
Photographer: Jean-Guy Kérouac

Close-up of brushstroke in oil paint
Photo credit: Sean Weaver, Art Gallery of Ontario

Thomson, Tom Canadian 1877–1917
A Rapid, 1915
oil on panel; 21.6 x 26.7 cm
Art Gallery of Ontario, Toronto
Gift of Mr. and Mrs. Lawren S. Harris, Toronto, 1927; 864

Watson, Homer Canadian 1855–1936
Haymaking, the Last Load, c. 1891
oil on canvas; 53.2 x 80.1 cm
Collection of the Art Gallery of Hamilton
Gift of the North American Life Assurance Co., 1963

Carmichael, Franklin Canadian 1890–1945
North Shore, Lake Superior, 1927
oil on canvas; 102.8 x 122.5 cm
Art Gallery of Ontario, Toronto
Purchased with the assistance of the Government of Canada through the Cultural Property Export and Import Act, 1991; 91/33

O'Brien, Lucius Canadian 1832–1899
Through the Rocky Mountains, a pass on the Canadian Highway, 1887
watercolour on paper; 101.6 x 69.8 cm
Private Collection, Toronto
Photo: Courtesy Art Gallery of Ontario

Harris, Lawren S. Canadian 1885–1970
Isolation Peak, c. 1931
oil on canvas; 107.3 x 128 cm
Hart House Permanent Collection, University of Toronto
By permission of the family of Lawren S. Harris

The Group from Coast to Coast (pages 14/15)

Compass
Photo credit: Sean Weaver, Art Gallery of Ontario

Harris, Lawren S. Canadian 1885–1970
Icebergs, Davis Strait, 1930
oil on canvas; 121.9 x 152.4 cm
Gift of Mr. and Mrs. H. Spencer Clark
McMichael Canadian Art Collection; 1971.17
By permission of the family of Lawren S. Harris

Harris, Lawren S. Canadian 1885–1970
Maligne Lake, Jasper Park, 1924
oil on canvas; 122.8 x 152.8 cm
National Gallery of Canada, Ottawa
Purchased, 1928; 3541
By permission of the family of Lawren S. Harris

Harris, Lawren S. Canadian 1885–1970
Beaver Swamp, Algoma, 1920
oil on canvas; 120.7 x 141.0 cm
Art Gallery of Ontario, Toronto
Gift of Ruth Massey Tovell, Toronto, in memory of Harold Murchison Tovell, 1953; 53/12

Jackson, A.Y. Canadian 1882–1974
Winter, Charlevoix County, 1932
oil on canvas; 63.5 x 81.3 cm
Art Gallery of Ontario, Toronto
Purchase, 1933; 2156

Lismer, Arthur Canadian 1885–1969
Nova Scotia Fishing Village, 1930
oil on canvas; 92.5 x 107.4 cm
National Gallery of Canada, Ottawa
Purchased, 1936; 4280

Painting in the North (pages 16/17)

A.Y. Jackson's paint box
Art Gallery of Ontario
Photo credit: Sean Weaver, Art Gallery of Ontario

Mosquitoes
David Wistow

A.Y. Jackson, Frank Johnston and Lawren Harris on the Algoma boxcar
McMichael Canadian Art Collection Archives

Franklin Carmichael sketching at Grace Lake 1935
Photo: Joachim Gauthier
McMichael Canadian Art Collection Archives

Lismer, Arthur Canadian 1885–1969
Beasts of Burden, 1927 (detail)
graphite on paper; 18.4 x 23.5 cm
McMichael Canadian Art Collection
Gift of Mrs. James H. Knox; 1984.27.9

Thomson, Tom Canadian 1877–1917
Northern River, c. 1914–1915
oil on canvas; 115.1 x 102.0 cm
National Gallery of Canada, Ottawa
Purchased, 1915; 1055

How Did the Group Paint? (pages 18/19)

Paintbrush and paint
Photo credit: Sean Weaver, Art Gallery of Ontario

Thomson, Tom Canadian 1877–1917
Sketch for "The Jack Pine," c. 1916
oil on wood panel; 21.1 x 26.8 cm; 982.65
Courtesy of The Weir Foundation, Queenston, Ontario
Thomas Moore Photography, Toronto

Thomson, Tom Canadian 1877–1917
The Jack Pine, 1916–1917
oil on canvas; 127.9 x 139.8 cm
National Gallery of Canada, Ottawa
Purchased, 1918; 1519

A.Y. Jackson at Baffin Island, July, 1965
Courtesy Art Gallery of Ontario
Reproduced courtesy of Dr. Naomi Jackson Groves

Studio Building
National Gallery of Canada, Ottawa

A.Y. Jackson in his studio
Photo: Jock Carroll for WEEKEND
Courtesy Art Gallery of Ontario
Reproduced courtesy of Dr. Naomi Jackson Groves

The Mystery of Tom Thomson (pages 20/21)

Fishing wire
Photo credit: Sean Weaver, Art Gallery of Ontario

Tom Thomson
National Gallery of Canada, Ottawa

Thomson, Tom Canadian 1877–1917
Autumn Foliage, 1915
oil on panel; 21.6 x 26.7 cm
Art Gallery of Ontario, Toronto
Gift from the Reuben and Kate Leonard Canadian Fund; 852

Tom Thomson on Tea Lake Dam
National Gallery of Canada, Ottawa

Thomson's monument at Canoe Lake, Algonquin Park
National Gallery of Canada, Ottawa

Painting a Portrait (pages 22/23)

Varley, F.H. Canadian 1881–1969
Self-portrait, 1919
oil on canvas; 60.5 x 51.0 cm
National Gallery of Canada, Ottawa
Purchased, 1936; 4272
Reproduced courtesy of Mrs. Kathleen McKay/Estate/F.H. Varley Estate

Oil paint
Photo credit: Sean Weaver, Art Gallery of Ontario

Varley, F.H. Canadian 1881–1969
Vera, 1931
oil on canvas; 61.0 x 50.6 cm
National Gallery of Canada, Ottawa
Vincent Massey Bequest, 1968; 15559
Reproduced courtesy of Mrs. Kathleen McKay/Estate/F.H. Varley Estate

Varley, F.H. Canadian 1881–1969
Portrait of Vincent Massey, 1920
oil on canvas; 120.7 x 141 cm
Hart House Permanent Collection, University of Toronto
Reproduced courtesy of Mrs. Kathleen McKay/Estate/F.H. Varley Estate

Lismer, Arthur Canadian 1885–1969
Self Portrait, 1924
oil on board; 91.0 x 76.3 cm
McMichael Canadian Art Collection
Gift of Mr. A.J. Latner; 1971.10

Holgate, Edwin Canadian 1892–1977
The Lumberjack, 1924
oil on canvas; 64.8 x 56.6 cm
(25¹/₂ x 21¹/₂ in.)
Collection of Gallery Lambton, Sarnia, Ontario
Gift of the Sarnia Women's Conservation Art Association, 1956

Other Group of Seven Projects (pages 24/25)

Carmichael, Franklin Canadian 1890–1945
Illustrations and design by Carmichael; Sampson Matthews Ltd., Toronto for Ford Motor Co. of Canada Ltd.
Her Personal Car, 1926
lithography on paper; 30.2 x 22.6 cm
Art Gallery of Ontario, Toronto. Collection of The Edward P. Taylor Research Library and Archives

Jackson, A.Y. Canadian 1882–1974
A Little Book of Bird Songs book cover
Reproduced courtesy of Dr. Naomi Jackson Groves

MacDonald, J.E.H. Canadian 1873–1932
Poster, 1914
Ontario College of Art and Design Permanent Collection

Thomson, Jackson, Lismer and
MacDonald
Cottage murals
The MacCallum Bequest of Paintings
National Gallery of Canada, Ottawa
Photo credit: John Evans Photography
Ltd.; 1328

Jackson, A.Y. Canadian 1882–1974
View of Kokanee Park Car January 1955
Kokanee Glacier Provincial Park
British Columbia
Canadian Pacific Archives, B.3864.1
Reproduced courtesy of Dr. Naomi
Jackson Groves

St. Anne's Church ceiling, 1923
Photo credit: Peter Coffman

Did You Know … ? (pages 26/27)
Thomson, Tom Canadian 1877–1917
A Northern Lake, 1912–13
oil on canvas; 69.9 x 101.6 cm
Art Gallery of Ontario, Toronto
Gift of the Government of the Province of
Ontario, 1972; 72/25

Tom Thomson die symbol
Thoreau MacDonald
National Gallery of Canada, Ottawa; 1531

Tom Thomson forgery
National Gallery of Canada, Ottawa

A.Y. Jackson in uniform, 1919
National Gallery of Canada, Ottawa
Reproduced courtesy of Dr. Naomi
Jackson Groves

Varley, F.H. Canadian 1881–1969
Head of a Girl, c. 1936
charcoal and charcoal wash on wove
paper; 23.9 x 23.1 cm
National Gallery of Canada, Ottawa
Purchased, 1936; 4305
Reproduced courtesy of Mrs. Kathleen
McKay/Estate/F.H. Varley Estate

FitzGerald, Lionel LeMoine Canadian
1890–1956
Doc Snyder's House, 1931
oil on canvas; 74.9 x 85.1 cm
National Gallery of Canada, Ottawa
Gift of P.D. Ross, Ottawa, 1932; 3993

**Differing Opinions About the Group
(pages 28/29)**
Harris, Lawren S. Canadian 1885–1970
Lake Superior, c. 1924
oil on canvas; 101.7 x 127.3 cm
Art Gallery of Ontario, Toronto
Bequest of Charles S. Band, Toronto, 1970;
69/121
By permission of the family of Lawren S.
Harris

Jackson, A.Y. Canadian 1882–1974
Terre Sauvage, 1913
oil on canvas; 128.8 x 154.4 cm
National Gallery of Canada, Ottawa; 4351
Reproduced courtesy of Dr. Naomi
Jackson Groves

Lismer, Arthur Canadian 1885–1969
Portrait of Hector Charlesworth,
c. 1931–1933
pen and blue ink on wove paper
12.8 x 10.2 cm
National Gallery of Canada, Ottawa
Gift of F. Maud Brown, Ottawa, 1970; 15937

MacDonald, J.E.H. Canadian 1873–1932
The Tangled Garden, 1916
oil on beaverboard; 121.4 x 152.4 cm
National Gallery of Canada, Ottawa
Gift of W.M. Southam, F.N. Southam, and
H.S. Southam, 1937, in memory of their
brother Richard Southam; 4291

MacDonald, J.E.H. Canadian 1873–1932
The Elements, 1916
oil on board; 71.1 x 91.8 cm
Art Gallery of Ontario, Toronto
Gift of Dr. Lorne Pierce, Toronto, 1958, in
memory of Edith Chown Pierce
(1890–1954); 57/45

**What Do People See in Works by the
Group of Seven? (pages 30/31)**
J.E.H. MacDonald c.1930
McMichael Canadian Art Collection
Archives

Arthur Lismer and Tom Thomson
Canoe Lake, Algonquin Park 1914
McMichael Canadian Art Collection
Archives

MacDonald, J.E.H. Canadian 1873–1932
The Beaver Dam, 1919
oil on canvas; 81.6 x 86.7 cm
Art Gallery of Ontario, Toronto
Gift from the Reuben and Kate Leonard
Canadian Fund, 1926; 840

Other Artists (pages 32/33)
Emily Carr with pets, c.1931
Courtesy Art Gallery of Ontario

Milne, David B. Canadian 1882–1953
Painting Place, No. 3, 1930
oil on canvas; 51.3 x 66.4 cm
National Gallery of Canada, Ottawa
Vincent Massey Bequest, 1968; 15520
By permission of the Milne Estate

Carr, Emily Canadian 1871–1945
Scorned as Timber, Beloved of the Sky,
1935
oil on canvas; 112.0 x 68.9 cm
Vancouver Art Gallery/Trevor Mills;
VAG 42.3.15
Reproduction courtesy of the Emily Carr
Trust

Clark, Paraskeva Canadian 1898–1986
Petroushka, 1937
oil on canvas; 122.4 x 81.9 cm
National Gallery of Canada, Ottawa
Purchased, 1976; 18624
Reproduction with permission of Clive and
Benedict Clark

Brooker, Bertram Canadian 1888–1955
Sound Assembling, 1928
oil on canvas; 112.3 x 91.7 cm
Collection of the Winnipeg Art Gallery;
(Accession #: L-80)
Photo: Ernest Mayer, Winnipeg Art Gallery
Reproduction courtesy of Phyllis Brooker
Smith

Loring, Frances Norma Canadian
1887–1968
Goal Keeper, 1935
plaster, patina; 242.0 cm
Art Gallery of Ontario, Toronto
Gift of the Estates of Frances Loring and
Florence Wyle, 1983; 83/62

**Learn About Nature with the Group of
Seven (pages 34/35)**
Varley, F.H. Canadian 1881–1969
Stormy Weather, Georgian Bay, 1921
oil on canvas; 132.6 x 162.8 cm
National Gallery of Canada, Ottawa
Purchased, 1921
Reproduced courtesy of Mrs. Kathleen
McKay/Estate/F.H. Varley Estate; 1814

Thomson, Tom Canadian 1877–1917
Tamaracks c.1916
oil on panel; 21.3 x 26.7
McMichael Canadian Art Collection
Gift of Mr. R.A. Laidlaw; 1968.12

Thomson, Tom Canadian 1877–1917
The West Wind, 1917
oil on canvas; 120.7 x 137.2 cm
Art Gallery of Ontario, Toronto
Gift of the Canadian Club of Toronto, 1926;
784

Thomson, Tom Canadian 1877–1917
Grey Sky, 1914
oil on wood; 22.5 x 27.3 cm
National Gallery of Canada, Ottawa
Purchased, 1918; 1531

Johnston, Frank Canadian 1888–1949
The Fire Ranger, c. 1920
oil on canvas; 123.0 x 153.2 cm
National Gallery of Canada, Ottawa
Purchased, 1921; 1823
With permission of Wenawae Stevenson

Thomson, Tom Canadian 1877–1917
Northern Lights
oil on cardboard
Collection of the Tom Thomson Memorial
Art Gallery & Museum of Fine Art
Gift of Mrs. J.G. Henry

**Landscape Art Since the Group
(pages 36/37)**
Chambers, Jack Canadian 1931–1978
Lombardo Avenue, 1973
From the collection of the Canada Council
for the Arts, Art Bank
Reproduction of *Lombardo Avenue*
courtesy of the Estate of Jack Chambers

Colville, Alex Canadian 1920–
Woman, Dog and Canoe, 1982
screenprint on paper (serigraph);
44.0 x 71.1 (sheet)
Art Gallery of Ontario, Toronto
Gift of Dr. Helen J. Dow, Ottawa, 1993;
94/133
Reproduction courtesy of Alex Colville

Ewen, Paterson Canadian 1925–
Northern Lights, 1973
acrylic, oil, dry pigment on galvanized
steel and gouged plywood;
167.5 x 244.0 cm
Art Gallery of Ontario, Toronto
Purchase, Margaret P. Nesbitt
Endowment, 1973; 73/34
Copyright 1973 Paterson Ewen

Iskowitz, Gershon Canadian 1921–1988
Little Orange Painting II, 1974
oil on canvas; 177.8 x 165.1 cm
Art Gallery of Ontario, Toronto
Gift of Beverly and Boris Zerafa, 1975;
75/60

N.E. THING CO. Canadian 1936–
Bagged Landscape with Water, 1966
inflated vinyl; water; food colouring;
198.1 x 137.2 cm
Art Gallery of Ontario, Toronto
Gift of Mr. and Mrs. H.A. Malcolmson,
1985; 85/616
Reproduction courtesy of Iain Baxter

Remembering the Group (pages 38/39)
Robert and Signe McMichael
Photo: Janis Kraulis

Harris, Lawren S. Canadian 1885–1970
Montreal River, c. 1920
oil on board; 27.0 x 34.7 cm
McMichael Canadian Art Collection
Gift of the Founders, Robert and Signe
McMichael; 1966.16.77
By permission of the family of Lawren S.
Harris

Arthur Lismer
Photo gift of Marjorie Lismer Bridges
McMichael Canadian Art Collection
Archives

Lismer, Arthur Canadian 1885–1969
Pine Wrack, 1939
watercolour; gouache on paper;
55.9 x 75.5 cm
McMichael Canadian Art Collection
Gift of the Founders, Robert and Signe
McMichael; 1966.16.111

**So You Want to Own a Group of Seven
Painting (pages 40/41)**
Sotheby's catalogues and auction notice,
with gavel
Photo credit: Sean Weaver, Art Gallery of
Ontario

Conservators
Courtesy Art Gallery of Ontario

Harris, Lawren S. Canadian 1885–1970
The Corner Store, 1912
oil on canvas; 88.5 x 66.2 cm
Art Gallery of Ontario, Toronto
Bequest of Mary Gordon Nesbitt, Toronto,
1992; 92/113
By permission of the family of Lawren S.
Harris

The Artists (pages 42/45)
Franklin Carmichael
National Gallery of Canada, Ottawa
Photo credit: M.O. Hammond

A.J. Casson, 1930
Courtesy Art Gallery of Ontario
The Edward P. Taylor Research Library
and Archives

Lionel LeMoine FitzGerald, 1930
National Gallery of Canada, Ottawa
Photo credit: M.O. Hammond; 035106

Lawren Stewart Harris, c. 1925–30
National Gallery of Canada, Ottawa
Photo credit: M.O. Hammond

Edwin Holgate
National Gallery of Canada, Ottawa

A. Y. Jackson
Baie St. Paul 1923
McMichael Canadian Art Collection
Archives
Reproduced courtesy of Dr. Naomi
Jackson Groves

Frank Johnston (1888–1949)
Courtesy Art Gallery of Ontario

Arthur Lismer, 1934
Courtesy Art Gallery of Ontario

J.E.H. MacDonald
Courtesy Art Gallery of Ontario

Frederick Horsman Varley, c. 1921
National Gallery of Canada, Ottawa

Tom Thomson, c. 1900
National Gallery of Canada, Ottawa
Portrait by E. Tucker, Owen Sound, Ontario

Index

The Group of Seven